101 KNOCK KNOCK JOKES

VOLUME 1

THE HENNESSY KIDS

Featured Artwork by
JEB BONAGUA

THE HENNESSY ENTERTAINMENT COMPANY

101 Knock Knock Jokes / by The Hennessy Kids

ISBN 978-1-989621-00-4 (Print)

ISBN 978-1-989621-01-1 (E-book)

1. Wit and humor, Juvenile. 2. English wit and humor. I. The Hennessy Kids, author

The Hennessy Entertainment Company | HennessyEnt.com |

Copyright © 2022 by The Hennessy Entertainment Company

All rights reserved.

No part of this book may be reproduced in any form or by any electronic or mechanical means, including information storage and retrieval systems, without written permission from the author, except for the use of brief quotations in a book review.

For Diane, Judith, Carole, and all our friends at the Bathurst Public Library.

FEATURED ARTWORK #1

Artwork by Jeb Bonagua.

1

KNOCK KNOCK JOKES

Knock, knock.
    Who's there?
    A little old lady.
    A little old lady who?
    Cool, I didn't know you could yodel.

Knock, knock.
    Who's there?
    Adore.
    Adore who?
    Adore is between you and me so please open up!

Knock, knock.
    Who's there?
    Boo.
    Boo who?
    Don't cry.

Knock, knock.
>Who's there?
>A pile up.
>A pile up who?
>Eww, that's just gross.

Knock, knock.
>Who's there?
>Cockle doodle.
>Cockle doodle who?
>Guess it's time to wake up.

Knock, knock.
>Who's there?
>Control Freak.
>Contro—
>Okay, now you say, "Control freak who?"

Knock, knock.
>Who's there?
>Interrupting zombie.
>Inter—
>BRAAAAAAINS.

Knock, knock.
>Who's there?
>Interrupting sloth.
>Interrupting sloth who?
>(Count to 5 silently, then): Slooooooooth.

Knock, knock.
   Who's there?
   Cotton.
   Cotton who?
   Cotton the door, please open it and let me out.

Knock, knock.
   Who's there?
   Cows go.
   Cows go who?
   No, cows go moo.

Knock, knock.
   Who's there?
   Déjà.
   Déjà who?
   Knock, knock.

Knock, knock.
   Who's there?
   Dime.
   Dime who?
   Dime for another knock-knock joke.

Knock, knock.
   Who's there?
   Disguise.
   Disguise who?
   Disguise falling, disguise falling.

Knock, knock.
    Who's there?
    Dishes
    Dishes who?
    Dishes the police, open up!

Knock, knock.
    Who's there?
    Dismay.
    Dismay who?
    Dismay seem funny to you, but I don't like it.

Knock, knock.
    Who's there?
    Doctor.
    Doctor who?
    No, no, just the doctor.

Knock, knock.
    Who's there?
    Ears.
    Ears who?
    Ears another knock-knock joke for you.

Knock, knock.
    Who's there?
    Europe.
    Europe who?
    Now that's just rude.

Knock, knock.
    Who's there?
    Gruesome.
    Gruesome who?
    Gruesome carrots in my garden.

Knock, knock.
    Who's there?
    Haven.
    Haven who?
    Haven you heard enough of these knock-knock jokes?

Knock, knock.
    Who's there?
    Hike.
    Hike who?
    I didn't know you liked Japanese poetry!

Knock, knock.
    Who's there?
    Honeybee.
    Honeybee who?
    Honeybee a dear and open up will you?

Knock, knock.
    Who's there?
    Howl.
    Howl who?
    Howl you know if you don't open the door?

Knock, knock.
> Who's there?
> Ice cream soda.
> Ice cream soda who?
> Ice scream soda whole house knows I'm at the door.

Knock, knock.
> Who's there?
> Icing.
> Icing who?
> Icing so loudly so everyone can hear me!

Knock, knock.
> Who's there?
> Icy.
> Icy who?
> Icy no reason for you to keep me outside.

Knock, knock.
> Who's there?
> June.
> June who?
> June know how long I've been knocking out here?

Knock, knock.
> Who's there?
> Lass.
> Lass who?
> That's what cowboys use.

Knock, knock.
    Who's there?
    Moustache.
    Moustache who?
    Moustache you a question, but I'll shave it for later!

Knock, knock.
    Who's there?
    Needle.
    Needle who?
    Needle little help getting in the door!

Knock, knock.
    Who's there?
    Nuisance.
    Nuisance who?
    What's nuisance yesterday?

Knock, knock.
    Who's there?
    Nun.
    Nun who?
    Nun of your business!

Knock, knock.
    Who's there?
    Owls say.
    Owls say who?
    Yes, they do.

Knock, knock.
   Who's there?
   Unaware.
   Unaware who?
   Unaware is the first thing you put on in the morning.

Knock, knock.
   Who's there?
   Panther.
   Panther who?
   Panther what you can put on after your unaware.

Knock, knock.
   Who's there?
   Police.
   Police who?
   Police open the door and let me in.

Knock, knock.
   Who's there?
   Radio.
   Radio who?
   Radio not, here I come.

Knock, knock.
   Who's there?
   Razor.
   Razor who?
   Razor hand if you know the answer.

Knock, knock.
   Who's there?
   Repeat.
   Repeat who?
   Who, who, who.

Knock, knock.
   Who's there?
   Rita.
   Rita who?
   Rita lot of these jokes to your friends.

Knock, knock.
   Who's there?
   Santa.
   Santa who?
   Santa text message telling you to open the door.

Knock, knock.
   Who's there?
   Says.
   Says who?
   Says me, that's who!

Knock, knock.
   Who's there?
   Smellmop.
   Smellmop who?
   Ewww, no thanks.

Knock, knock.

Who's there?
Snow.
Snow who?
Snow use, I forgot my name again.

Knock, knock.
Who's there?
Spell.
Spell who?
W-H-O.

Knock, knock.
Who's there?
Stopwatch.
Stopwatch who?
Stopwatch you're doing and open the door.

Knock, knock.
Who's there?
Tank.
Tank who?
You're welcome, you're welcome.

Knock, knock.
Who's there?
Tennis.
Tennis who?
Tennis the number after nine.

Knock, knock.
　Who's there?
　To.
　To who?
　No, it's to whom!

Knock, knock.
　Who's there?
　Trigger.
　Trigger who?
　Trigger treat.

Knock, knock.
　Who's there?
　Voodoo.
　Voodoo who?
　Voodoo you think you are, asking me so many questions?

Knock, knock.
　Who's there?
　Waddle.
　Waddle who?
　Waddle you give me to stop knocking on your door?

Knock, knock.
　Who's there?
　Want.
　Want who?
　Want, who ... three, four, five!

THE HENNESSY KIDS

Knock, knock.
  Who's there?
  Water.
  Water who?
  Water you waiting for, open the door.

Knock, knock.
  Who's there?
  Wire.
  Wire who?
  Wire you always asking, "Who's there?"

Knock, knock.
  Who's there?
  Woo.
  Woo who?
  Don't get too excited, it's only a joke.

Knock, knock.
  Who's there?
  Wooden shoe.
  Wooden shoe who?
  Wooden shoe like to open the door now?

Knock, knock.
  Who's there?
  A herd.
  A herd who?
  A herd you were home so I came over.

Knock, knock.
>Who's there?
>Canoe.
>Canoe who?
>Canoe come out and play?

2
NAME KNOCK KNOCK JOKES

Knock, knock.
    Who's there?
    Al.
    Al who?
    Al come in if you open the door.

Knock, knock.
    Who's there?
    Mikey.
    Mikey who?
    Mikey is stuck in the lock.

Knock, knock.
    Who's there?
    Nadya.
    Nadya who?
    Nadya head if you understand.

Knock, knock.
>Who's there?
>Theodore.
>Theodore who?
>Theodore wasn't opened so I knocked.

Knock, knock.
>Who's there?
>Candice.
>Candice who?
>Candice joke get any worse?!

Knock, knock.
>Who's there?
>Arch.
>Arch who?
>Bless you. Are you catching a cold?

Knock, knock.
>Who's there?
>Nicholas.
>Nicholas who?
>A Nicholas is not much money these days.

Knock, knock.
>Who's there?
>Watson.
>Watson who?
>Not much, what's new with you?

Knock, knock.
    Who's there?
    Doris.
    Doris who?
    Doris not open, that's why I'm knocking.

Knock, knock.
    Who's there?
    Dwayne.
    Dwayne who?
    Dwayne the bathtub, I'm dwowning.

Knock, knock.
    Who's there?
    Alex.
    Alex who?
    Alex-plain when you open the door!

Knock, knock.
    Who's there?
    Amos.
    Amos who?
    A mosquito.

Knock, knock.
    Who's there?
    Juno.
    Juno who?
    Juno what time it is?

THE HENNESSY KIDS

Knock, knock.
    Who's there?
    Emma.
    Emma who?
    Emma gonna have to knock again, or you gonna let me in?

Knock, knock.
    Who's there?
    Anita.
    Anita who?
    Anita drink of water, I'm really thirsty.

Knock, knock.
    Who's there?
    Annie
    Annie who?
    Annie thing you can do I can better.

Knock, knock.
    Who's there?
    Lena.
    Lena who?
    Lena a little closer, and I'll tell you another joke!

Knock, knock.
    Who's there?
    Leon.
    Leon who?
    Leon me when you're not strong!

Knock, knock.
>   Who's there?
>   Stan.
>   Stan who?
>   Stan back, I'm kicking the door down.

# FEATURED ARTWORK #2

THE HENNESSY KIDS

Artwork by Jeb Bonagua.

3

ANIMAL KNOCK-KNOCK JOKES

Knock, knock.
    Who's there?
    Champ.
    Champ who?
    Champoo the dog, he was sprayed by a skunk!

Knock, knock.
    Who's there?
    Goat.
    Goat who?
    Goat to your room.

Knock, knock.
    Who's there?
    Dude.
    Dude who?
    Dude-doo in the yard, need to scoop it up.

Knock, knock.
  Who's there?
  Kanga.
  Kanga who?
  I think you mean kangaroo.

Knock, knock.
  Who's there?
  Zachary Oswald Turtle the Third.
  Zachary Oswald Turtle the Third who?
  How many Zachary Oswald Turtle the Thirds do you know?

Knock. Knock.
  Who's there?
  Poodle.
  Poodle who?
  Poodle lot of ketchup on my hot dog, please.

4

FOOD KNOCK KNOCK JOKES

Knock, knock.
 Who's there?
 Arthur.
 Arthur who?
 Arthur any tasty snacks in there? I'm hungry.

Knock, knock.
 Who's there?
 Gorilla.
 Gorilla who?
 Gorilla cheese sandwich.

Knock, knock.
 Who's there?
 Lettuce.
 Lettuce who?
 Lettuce is, it's raining out here.

Knock, knock.
  Who's there?
  Irish stew.
  Irish stew who?
  Irish stew in the name of the law.

Knock, knock.
  Who's there?
  Pete.
  Pete who?
  Pete-za delivery.

Knock, knock.
  Who's there?
  Cabbage.
  Cabbage who?
  You expect a cabbage to have a last name?

Knock, knock.
  Who's there?
  Cash.
  Cash who?
  No, thanks, I'm allergic to nuts.

Knock, knock.
  Who's there?
  Figs.
  Figs who?
  Figs the doorbell!

Knock, knock.
    Who's there?
    Butter.
    Butter who?
    Butter let me in.

Knock, knock.
    Who's there?
    Weiner.
    Weiner who?
    Weiner you going to let me in?

Knock, knock.
    Who's there?
    Sweden.
    Sweden who?
    Sweden sour chicken!

Knock, knock.
    Who's there?
    Quiche.
    Quiche who?
    Can I have a hug and a quiche?

Knock, knock.
    Who's there?
    Orange.
    Orange who?
    Orange you going to let me in?

Knock, knock.
　　Who's there?
　　Turnip.
　　Turnip who?
　　Turnip the radio, that's my favourite song.

Knock, knock.
　　Who's there?
　　Avocado.
　　Avocado who?
　　Avocado cold.

FEATURED ARTWORK #3

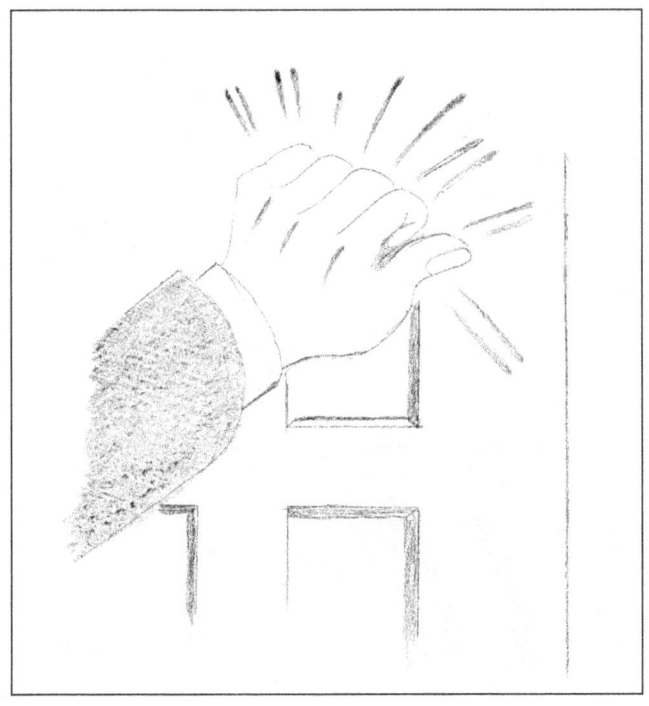

Artwork by Jeb Bonagua

5

STAR WARS KNOCK KNOCK JOKES

Knock, knock.
    Who's there?
    Yoda.
    Yoda who?
    Yoda best!

Knock, knock.
    Who's there?
    Art.
    Art who?
    Art-2-D-2.

Knock, knock.
    Who's there?
    Luke.
    Luke who?
    Luke out - here comes another knock knock joke.

THE HENNESSY KIDS

Knock, Knock.
 Who's there?
 Ahsoka.
 Ahsoka who?
 Ahsoka my dishes before I wash them.

6

YOUR FAVOURITE JOKE

What is your favourite knock knock joke that isn't in this book?

Send it to us at thehennessykids@gmail.com, and we'll look to share it online with all our friends.

ACKNOWLEDGMENTS

Special thank you to Jeb Bonagua for sharing his drawings.

Thank you for reading our book! We hope you enjoyed it. Please tell these jokes to your friends and family and make more people happy.

ABOUT THE AUTHORS

The Hennessy Kids think the world would be better with more smiles.

Want to know when our new books are available? Sign up for our **Fun Stuff With Heart** newsletter at HennessyEnt.com!

BOOKS BY THE HENNESSY KIDS

101 Halloween Jokes

101 Christmas Jokes

101 Pet Jokes

101 Knock Knock Jokes, Vol. 1

101 Nature Jokes

101 Food Jokes

www.ingramcontent.com/pod-product-compliance
Lightning Source LLC
Chambersburg PA
CBHW071255070526
44583CB00017B/2482